BLS WORKING PAPERS

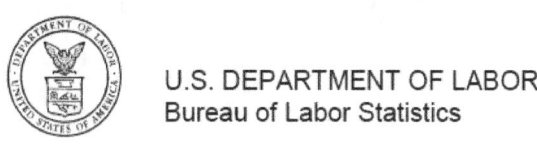

U.S. DEPARTMENT OF LABOR
Bureau of Labor Statistics

OFFICE OF EMPLOYMENT RESEARCH AND
PROGRAM DEVELOPMENT

The Impact of Worker and Establishment-level Characteristics on Male-Female
Wage Differentials: Evidence from Danish Matched Employee-Employer Data

Nabanita Datta Gupta, Aarhus School of Business, DK
Donna S. Rothstein, U.S. Bureau of Labor Statistics

Working Paper 347
October 2001

We thank Ronald Ehrenberg, Tor Ericsson, Erica Groshen, Judith Hellerstein, Michael Horrigan, Ronald Oaxaca, Brooks Pierce, and Paul Bingley for comments and discussions on an earlier draft. We thank CLS (pay and performance project) and Morten V. Rasmussen and Soren D. Anderson for competent research assistance. The views expressed are those of the authors and do not reflect the policies of the U.S. Bureau of Labor Statistics or the views of other staff members.

Revised, August 28, 2001
Comments welcome

The Impact of Worker and Establishment-level Characteristics on Male-Female Wage Differentials: Evidence from Danish Matched Employee-Employer Data

Nabanita Datta Gupta, *Aarhus School of Business, DK*

Donna S. Rothstein, *U.S. Bureau of Labor Statistics**

*We thank Ronald Ehrenberg, Tor Ericsson, Erica Groshen, Judith Hellerstein, Michael Horrigan, Ronald Oaxaca, Brooks Pierce, and Paul Bingley for comments and discussions on an earlier draft. We thank CLS (pay and performance project), and Morten V. Rasmussen and Soren D. Anderson for competent research assistance. The views expressed are those of the authors and do not reflect the policies of the BLS or the views of other BLS staff members.

Department of Economics, Aarhus School of Business, Fuglesangs Alle 20, DK-8210 Aarhus V, Denmark, phone: (+45) 89 48 64 21, fax: (+45) 86 15 51 75, email: ndg@asb.dk
Bureau of Labor Statistics, 2 Massachusetts Ave., NE, Suite 4945, Washington, DC 20212-0001, USA, phone: (+01) 202 691 7529, fax: (+01) 202 691 7425, email: rothstein_d@bls.gov

Abstract

This paper examines how the segregation of women into certain occupations, industries, establishments, and job cells impacts the gender wage differential of full-time, private sector workers in Denmark. We use matched employer and employee data that contain labor market information for the Danish population. This enables us to document, for the first time, the wage impacts of gender segregation at the level of establishment and job cell in Denmark. We estimate the wage effects of gender segregation at the above four levels through fixed effects or through controls for the proportion female within the four structures. We find that occupation has a much larger role than industry or establishment in accounting for the gender gap in full-time, private sector wages in Denmark. In addition, men and women earn different wages within job cells.

In this paper, we study the effects of levels of gender segregation on private sector wages in Denmark. We ask the following questions: Does the concentration of women in certain occupations, industries, establishments, or job cells (occupations within establishments) account for most of the gender gap in wages? Or, after controlling for segregation within these structures, along with human capital characteristics, does a large gender wage differential still remain?

To address these questions, we use matched employer and employee data of all full-time, private sector workers in Denmark. The data are from administrative records and include both person and establishment-level information. We estimate the wage impact of gender segregation at the occupation, industry, establishment, and job-cell levels through fixed effects or through controls for the proportion female within the four structures. Our results indicate that occupation has a much larger role than industry or establishment in accounting for the wage gap between men and women who work in the private sector. We also find a significant within job-cell gender wage differential.

Background

A starting point for our research is two papers that examined the impact of levels of gender segregation on the male-female wage gap in the United States. The first, Groshen (1991), uses cross-sectional data from five Bureau of Labor Statistics Industry Wage Surveys (IWS) that were fielded in the early1970s or 1980s.[1] The surveys are establishment-based and contain information on the gender and wages of full-time employees in a subset of occupations within

---

[1] The five industries are miscellaneous plastic products (1974), nonelectrical machinery (1983), life insurance (1980), banking (1980), and computer and data processing (1983).

the sampled establishments. Groshen estimates pooled wage equations that have controls for gender and the proportion female in occupation, establishment, and job cell.

In all five industries, Groshen (1991) finds that the femaleness of an occupation accounts for the largest proportion of the gender wage gap. In addition, she finds a negligible within job-cell gender wage differential. Groshen's results indicate that an understanding of the processes by which men and women are segregated into occupations, establishments, and job cells is an important key to understanding the underlying causes of the full-time gender gap in wages.

The second paper, by Bayard, et al. (2000), also uses data from the United States and obtains different results than Groshen (1991). Their data set, called the New Worker-Establishment Characteristics Database, matches persons (and person characteristics) from the 1990 Decennial Census long form with establishments from the 1990 Standard Statistical Establishment List (SSEL).[2] Bayard, et al. (2000) measure gender concentration at the occupation, industry, establishment, and job-cell levels. They find that these levels of gender segregation account for a large portion of the full-time gender gap in wages. However, they also find a significant within job-cell gender wage differential, even when including controls for human capital characteristics. The authors suggest that, in contrast to Groshen (1991), an understanding of the sources of within occupation, within establishment gender wage differences is important for explaining full-time male-female wage differentials.[3]

---

[2] The long form of the 1990 Decennial Census is filled out by one sixth of the households in the United States. Workers and establishments are matched based on detailed location and industry information in both data sets. Given various matching requirements, the authors note that their resulting matched sample is not a representative sample of U.S. workers.

[3] There is a substantial literature on the effect of occupational segregation on wages (see, for example, Macpherson and Hirsch (1995), Sorensen (1990)). Reilly and Wirjanto (1998) and Barth and Mastekaasa (1996) examine the wage impact of gender segregation at the establishment level. Blau (1977) uses 1970 data from three metropolitan statistical areas in the United States and documents sex-segregation by firm within occupational categories. Like Groshen (1991), Blau finds that the gender wage gaps within the select occupations examined appear to result from differences across firms rather than within firms.

As in the United States, Danish women entered the labor force in large numbers from the early 1960s onward. Educational opportunities opened up for women, and at the same time the public sector expanded to take up the care of children and elderly. In addition, the concern of pay parity between women and men began to be addressed. In 1973, the principle of equal pay was first established in Denmark in the context of collective bargaining agreements in the labor market. In 1976, the equal pay for equal work principle was enacted into law. Later, in 1986, the Danish Equal Pay Act was extended to require equal pay for work of equal value.[4] The change was made, in part, to conform to European Union directives.

Over the years, Danish women's labor force participation has increasingly come to resemble that of men's. A high proportion of women--73.5 percent in 1999--participate in the Danish labor force. And, as a percentage of the workforce, women have seen their relative shares increase in the skilled wage earner and salaried employee categories, and decrease in the unskilled wage earner category. However, gender segregation in employment in Denmark still remains relatively high.[5]

Our study examines the wage impacts of gender segregation at the occupation, industry, establishment, and job-cell levels for private sector, salaried workers in Denmark. Following Groshen (1991) and Bayard, et al. (2000), we estimate log of hourly wage equations that are pooled for men and women:

$$\ln w_{ijklm} = +\alpha f_i * O_j \ \beta + I_k \ \beta + E_l \ \beta_E + JC_m \beta_{JC} + X_{ijklm} \ \delta + \upsilon_{ijklm}$$

where, for individual i, working in occupation j, in industry k, establishment l, and job-cell m, w is the hourly wage and f is a dummy variable indicating gender (1=female, 0=male). O, I, E, and JC can either be fixed effects at the occupation, industry, establishment, and job-cell levels, or

---

[4] However, no systematic method of comparing work has been put in place.

measures of the proportion of workers that are female in each of the four labor market structures.[6] X is a standard vector of human capital characteristics.

In theory, both the wage equation with fixed effects and that with the proportion of workers who are female in each structure yield the identical coefficient on the female dummy variable (γ). The following explains why: The coefficient on the female indicator in a wage regression that includes a full set of job-cell dummy variables refers to female-male differences in pay for individuals that arise in the same job cells, that is, a *within*-job cell differential. The coefficients on the job cell dummy variables capture *between*-job-cell wage effects. Now, assume the job-cell fixed effects are replaced instead by the fraction of women working in the occupation, industry, establishment, and job cell. Any remaining differences across occupations, industries, establishments, and job cells that are not captured by the percent female variables (but were captured by the job cell fixed effects) must be orthogonal to being female. Thus they will not add any additional information that can explain the difference in the average pay between men and women within job cells. The between-job cell portion of the overall gender gap in wages describes how wages across each particular labor market structure vary with percent female in that structure. (See Welch (1990).) In this paper, however, the female dummy variable coefficients (γ) under the fixed effects and proportion female specifications may differ. As the next sections point out, this occurs because the sample used to define the proportion female variables is larger than that used for the wage regressions.

---

[5] See Linderoth, et al. (1997) and Asplund, et al. (1997).
[6] Note that job cell fixed effects also include fixed effects at the occupation, industry, and establishment levels.

Data and Descriptive Statistics

The data for our study are from the Integrated Database for Labour Market Research (Danish IDA). The IDA links information on employees and establishments drawn from the population register that contains labor market information on the entire Danish population (1980-1995). Thus there is no survey aspect as all the data are based on administrative registers.

Our analyses use data from 1983 and 1995, based on the full IDA. We thus span (at least part of) the same time period as Groshen (1991) and Bayard, et al. (2000). Further, these two years are on the same positions on the business cycle, recovery years, thereby minimizing differences in the results across years that arise due to business cycle effects.

We restrict our sample to individuals between 18 and 65, who are employed in the private sector, are not self-employed, work full time, have reliable wage information, and work in an establishment with at least 20 employees and in a job cell greater than 1.[7] We focus on salaried workers only. Rosholm and Smith (1996) find that wage functions are significantly different for salaried compared to manual workers. In addition, salaried workers are the largest occupational group in the Danish labor market in both the private and public sectors. The above restrictions lead to a sample size of 252,234 in 1983 and 313,099 in 1995 (see Appendix Table 1).

The dependent variable in this study is the log of hourly wage. The hourly wage measure in the IDA is created from an annual average based on earnings information supplied to the tax authorities and hours information based on employer contribution histories. IDA wage estimates have been shown to closely approximate industry wage statistics for white-collar workers (Larsen and Pedersen (1992)).

---

[7] The full-time definition is based upon annual hours of work. Annual hours of work are calculated from the supplementary pension payment, or ATP register, which contains information on annual mandatory employer payments. The ATP payment is a step-wise function of weekly or monthly hours. We define full time as working

In examining the gender gap in wages, it is important to include human capital characteristics. Years of education are the normed education lengths of a worker's completed education level (for example, high school).[8] About 2 to 3 percent of observations have missing education information. Thus we define a dummy variable for education missing that takes the value of 1 when information is missing (and years of education is set to 0) and 0 otherwise.

Our analyses include either age and age squared (as in Bayard, et al. (2000)) or experience and experience squared. The variable years of work experience is based on information in the ATP register, which goes back to 1964. For older workers in our sample who may have accumulated experience before 1964, we impute pre-1964 experience based on gender and cohort-specific full-time and part-time participation rates in the relevant years.

We estimate fixed effects models based on occupation, industry, establishment, or job cell. Detailed occupation is a 3-digit occupational code. The first digit refers to a worker's occupational position (for example, manager), the second digit refers to broad occupational levels (for example, clerical), and the third digit is further disaggregated occupational groupings (e.g. bookkeeper). Occupations with less than 20 workers have been aggregated up based on their occupational code.

Industry is based on a 2-digit industry code, which contains 52 industrial classifications. Establishment is the plant the individual is employed in during November of the particular year (1983, 1995). Job cell is defined as occupation within establishment. Job-cell fixed effects include fixed effects at the occupation, industry, and establishment levels.

Following Bayard, et al. (2000), we define four measures of gender concentration--the proportion female in occupation, industry, establishment, and job cell. We form these

---

1,166 or more annual hours--we combined ATP definitions with a selection criterion based on inspection of the bimodal hours distribution.

segregation measures using all full-time salaried employees in the private sector, thus avoiding the problem of measurement error that Bayard, et al. (2000) may encounter in their study.

Table 1 shows descriptive statistics for full-time, salaried, private sector workers in Denmark. The data indicate that the log difference in hourly wages between men and women is .386 in 1983. The gender wage gap decreases to .341 in 1995, a difference of .045. These estimates are in accordance with those found by Rosholm and Smith (1996) and Datta Gupta, Oaxaca, and Smith (1998), who point to a general stagnation of the gender wage gap in the 1980s and '90s.

Women have significantly less labor market experience than men. However, the gender gap in experience decreases substantially from 1983 to 1995. On average, female private sector workers are about 5.4 years younger than their male counterparts in 1983. This age difference is cut in half in 1995. Men's and women's educational levels are nearly even in 1995.

Job cells are the most segregated in Denmark, followed by occupation. Asplund, et al. (1997) find that occupational segregation in Denmark tends be relatively high compared to other Nordic countries. However, this is the first study to document the level of gender segregation at the establishment and job cell level in Denmark. In 1983, the average female worked in a job cell that is 69 percent female, whereas the average male worked in a job cell that is only 17 percent female. Between 1983 and 1995, women's participation in the full-time, private sector workforce significantly increased relative to men's. Although the average percent female in job cell remained about the same for women in 1995, it increased to 23 percent for men. Gender segregation is much less pronounced at the industry and establishment level in both 1983 and 1995.

---

[8] Results are very similar when dummy variables for education levels are used in the estimations.

Results

Does the concentration of women at the industry, occupation, establishment, or job-cell level account for most of the gender gap in wages? Or, after controlling for segregation within these structures, along with human capital characteristics, does a large gender wage differential still remain? Alternatively, as Groshen phrased the question in the title of her 1991 article: "Is it who you are, what you do, or where you work?" To address this question, we first analyze estimates from pooled log of hourly wage equations for 1983 and 1995 that include fixed effects at the occupation, industry, establishment, or job-cell level. We then examine results from specifications that substitute proportion female variables for the fixed effects. As discussed above, the results for the two types of specifications will differ because the proportion female variables are defined from the universe of full-time workers in Denmark. However, both sets of estimates do tell a similar story.

Table 2 displays, by year, the female coefficient estimates from 14 different specifications. In the first set of specifications, we exclude human capital characteristics, as in Groshen's (1991) analyses. In the second set of specifications, we include human capital characteristics, but use age and age squared rather than experience and experience squared, as in Bayard, et al. (2000). And, finally, in the third set of specifications, we substitute experience and experience squared for the age variables. Table 2 also presents the proportion of the gender wage gap accounted for by the sets of controls (= 1 − female coefficient/raw gender wage gap).

Looking first at the top line of Table 2, the mean difference in log hourly wages between women and men is -.386 in 1983 and -.341 in 1995. Estimations in the rows labeled (1) through (3) indicate that industry and establishment play a small role in accounting for the gender wage gap in Denmark. Occupation is key, accounting for almost 55 percent of the gap in 1983 (.547 =

1 -.175/.386) and over 50 percent in 1995. The job-cell fixed effects specification (row (4))
shows that within job cell, full-time female private sector workers earn about 16 percent less than
their male counterparts in both 1983 and 1995.[9]

We now turn to the two sets of human capital specifications. The human capital *only*
estimates (row (5), (10)) indicate that these characteristics account for almost 30 percent of the
gender wage gap in 1983, but only about 20 percent in 1995. This finding is not surprising,
given that the descriptive statistics in Table 1 show a decrease in the gender gap in human capital
characteristics in 1995 compared to 1983. As above, occupation (row (6), (11)) has a much
bigger role in accounting for the gender wage gap than industry (row (7), (12)) or establishment
(row (8), (13)). The addition of occupation fixed effects raises the explained portion of the gap
to 60 percent in 1983 and 50 percent in 1995. Again, the job-cell fixed effects estimates (row
(9), (14)) account for the highest proportion of the gender wage gap in both years.[10] And, as in
Bayard, et al. (2000), we find a significant within job-cell gender gap in wages.

The estimates in Table 2 point to the substantial role that occupation plays in accounting
for the wage gap between men and women, as found in Groshen (1991). In Table 3, we compare
specifications that use detailed occupation codes (as in Table 2) and less detailed occupation
codes (at the 2-digit level). The estimates of the effect of being female are fairly similar within
each specification type. They highlight the importance of occupation in explaining the gender
gap in private sector wages in Denmark.[11]

We now examine estimates from specifications that are more similar to those presented in
Groshen (1991) and Bayard, et al. (2000). These specifications include variables that measure

---

[9] The adjusted R-squared for specification (4) equals .58 in 1983 and .54 in 1995.
[10] The adjusted R-squared is over .66 in 1983 and about .62 percent in 1995.
[11] In contrast, Pedersen and Deding (2000) find that their broad 9-category measure of occupation does not explain a substantial portion of the gender wage gap for pooled salary and manual private sector workers in Denmark.

gender concentration at the various job levels rather than through fixed effects.[12] Tables 4 and 5

display estimates from pooled log of hourly wage equations that include the proportion female in

occupation, industry, establishment, and job cell as controls. Rows (1) through (4) show that,

when entered separately, the proportion female at each level has a negative impact on wages in

both 1983 and 1995. For example, an increase in the proportion female in occupation by 10

percent, reduces hourly wages by about 5 percent in both 1983 and 1995. As with the fixed

effects specifications, occupation plays a larger role than industry or establishment in accounting

for the gender wage gap. The estimates in row (5) indicate the substantial relative impact of the

proportion female in occupation on wages.[13] Overall, 58 percent of the gender wage gap is

accounted for in 1983 and 54 percent in 1995, leaving about 16 percent lower wages for women

relative to men in both years.[14]

Similar results are found in the specifications that include human capital characteristics.

In the fullest specification with experience (row (15)), almost 67 percent of the gender wage gap

is accounted for in 1983 and nearly 60 percent in 1995.[15][16] As in all of the results thus far,

"who" you are--that is, being female--is found to matter.

Recall that Groshen's (1991) work focuses on five industries, and is an industry-by-

industry analysis. Rather than trying to match these five industries in our data, we examine

results from three major industry groups in Denmark: manufacturing; wholesale and retail

---

[12] Bayard, et al. (2000) also show estimates from job-cell fixed effects specifications.

[13] Note that the proportion female variables, particularly occupation and job cell, are positively and sometimes highly correlated with each other (see Appendix Table 2).

[14] The adjusted R-squared for specification (5) equals .33 in 1983 and .27 in 1995.

[15] The adjusted R-squared is about .50 in 1983 and about .47 in 1995.

[16] Decompositions from gender-separate estimations show similar results—for example, using the male structure as the norm, in the row (15) specification about 70 percent of the gender wage gap is accounted for in 1983 and nearly 60 percent is accounted for in 1995.

trade; and financial intermediation and business activities.[17] In contrast to the United States, the manufacturing sector in Denmark did not experience a substantial decline between 1983 and 1995. As in the aggregate data, the percentage of female workers increased in the three sectors. In 1983, the manufacturing industry had only 27 percent of full-time, salaried workers who were female. The amount increases to 39 percent in 1995. Trade and financial intermediation have 35 and 40 percent female full-time workers in 1983, respectively. Trade increases to 43 percent and financial intermediation to 46 percent in 1995.

Tables 6, 7, and 8 display industry-specific estimates from a number of different specifications. The previous findings essentially hold by industry grouping. That is, occupation accounts for a substantial portion of the gender wage gap. And, even with human capital controls, within job-cell gender differentials in wages still remain. Being female is associated with earning about 15 percent lower wages within job cell in manufacturing in 1983 and 1995, about 16 (1983) to 20 percent (1995) lower wages in wholesale and retail trade, and about 13 (1983) to 17 percent (1995) lower wages in the financial intermediation industry.

---

[17] We thought the three general industry groupings would convey more information than a specific industry-by-industry analysis. We also could not precisely match Groshen's (1991) five industries, and it would be very difficult to match the selected occupations in Groshen's data with those available in the IDA.

Conclusion

In this paper, we examine how the segregation of women into certain occupations, industries, establishments, and job cells impacts the male-female wage differential of full-time, salaried, private sector workers in Denmark. To investigate this issue, we use the Integrated Database for Labour Market Research for the years 1983 and 1995. The data set is rich in both worker and establishment characteristics, and is based on registers that contain labor market information for the entire Danish population.

The gender differential in log hourly wages for full-time private sector workers is .386 in 1983. It falls to .341 in 1995, pointing to a general stagnation in the gender wage gap over this time period. Job cells are the most segregated in Denmark, followed by occupation. In 1983, full-time female employees work in a job cell that is 69 percent female and their male counterparts work in a job cell that is only 17 percent female. In 1995, this number remains about the same for women, but increases to 23 percent for men. Gender segregation is significantly less evident at the industry and establishment levels in both years.

We estimate log hourly wage equations with either fixed effects at the occupation, industry, establishment, or job-cell level or proportion female variables at these four levels. We find two key results, which are robust across various specifications. The first is that occupation differences account for much of the wage gap between men and women in Denmark. Groshen (1991) finds this with U.S. data from the early 1980s. The second is that even in the fullest specification, which includes human capital characteristics and job-cell fixed effects, men and women earn different wages within job cells. This coincides with results in Bayard, et al. (2000), who use 1990 U.S. matched employer and employee data.

Our results suggest that an investigation into the underlying reasons men and women enter different occupations is important for understanding one of the primary causes of the full-time gender gap in wages in Denmark. In addition, an assessment of why men and women are paid differently within jobs, within establishments would also provide insight into why a full-time gender wage differential has remained over the years.

References

Asplund, R., E. Barth, N. Smith, and E. Wadensjo. 1997. "The Male-Female Wage Gap in the Nordic Countries," in Westergard-Nielsen, N. (editor), *Wage Differentials in the Nordic Countries*. North Holland, Amsterdam.

Barth, Erling and Arne Mastekaasa. 1996. "Decomposing the Male/Female Wage Gap: Within and Between Establishment Differences." *Labour* 10 (2): 339-56.

Bayard, Kimberly, Judith Hellerstein, David Neumark, and Kenneth Troske. January 2000. "New Evidence on Sex Segregation and Sex Differences in Wages from Matched Employee-Employer Data." Mimeo. University of Maryland at College Park. (also, *N.B.E.R. Working Paper No. 7003*).

Blau, Francine. 1977. *Equal Pay in the Office*. Lexington, MA: D.C. Heath and Company.

Datta Gupta, Nabanita, Ronald L. Oaxaca, and Nina Smith. 1998. "Wage Dispersion, Public Sector Wages and the Stagnating Danish Gender Wage Gap." Centre for Labour Market and Social Research Working Paper 98-18.

Groshen, Erica L. 1991. "The Structure of the Female/Male Wage Differential: Is It Who You Are, What You Do, or Where You Work?" *Journal of Human Resources* 26 (3): 457-72.

Linderoth, Hans, Valdemar Smith, Niels Westergaard-Nielsen, and O. Kurt Geill. 1997. *Descriptive Economics*, translated excerpts from the 5th edition. Aarhus School of Business, Department of Economics, internal teaching material.

Macpherson, David A. and Barry T. Hirsch. 1995. "Wages and Gender Composition: Why Do Women's Jobs Pay Less?" *Journal of Labor Economics* 13 (3): 426-71.

Pedersen, Lisbeth and Mette Deding. 2000. "Wage Differences between Women and Men in Denmark" ("Lønforskelle mellem kvinder og mænd i Danmark") The Danish National Institute of Social Research (SFI).

Reilly, Kevin T. and Tony S. Wirjanto. 1998. "Does More Mean Less? The Male/Female Wage Gap and the Proportion of Females at the Establishment Level." Centre for Labour Market and Social Research Working Paper 98-04.

Rosholm, M. and N. Smith. 1996. "The Danish Gender Wage Gap in the 1980s: A Panel Data Study." *Oxford Economic Papers* 48: 254-79.

Sorensen, Elaine. 1990. "The Crowding Hypothesis and Comparable Worth." *Journal of Human Resources* 25 (1): 55-89.

Welch, Finis. August 1990. "The Comparable Worth Pay Regression." Unicom Research Corporation, Santa Monica, CA, mimeo.

Table 1. Descriptive Statistics: Full-time, Salaried, Private Sector Workers in Denmark

Variable Name	1983		1995	
	Males	Females	Males	Females
Hourly wage	84.877	55.860	105.920	72.436
	(37.065)	(15.699)	(50.969)	(23.753)
Ln hourly wage	4.371	3.985	4.577	4.236
	(.364)	(.277)	(.402)	(.303)
Human Capital				
Years of education	12.265	11.447	12.876	12.220
	(2.501)	(2.272)	(2.330)	(2.107)
Age	40.615	35.188	41.329	38.592
	(10.952)	(11.030)	(10.486)	(10.185)
Age sq./100	17.696	13.598	18.180	15.931
	(9.274)	(8.600)	(8.809)	(8.132)
Experience	19.863	11.865	19.598	15.545
	(11.620)	(7.093)	(10.840)	(8.251)
Experience sq./100	5.295	1.911	5.016	3.097
	(5.268)	(2.038)	(4.848)	(2.821)
Province	.480	.424	.539	.495
	(.500)	(.494)	(.498)	(.500)
Occupation, Industry, And Establishment				
Proportion female in occupation	.205	.634	.284	.638
	(.241)	(.233)	(.257)	(.212)
Proportion female in industry	.315	.397	.395	.462
	(.110)	(.166)	(.115)	(.137)
Proportion female in establishment	.332	.387	.402	.463
	(.095)	(.122)	(.105)	(.121)
Proportion female in job cell	.172	.690	.234	.700
	(.242)	(.233)	(.267)	(.220)
Ln establishment size	5.084	4.912	5.097	4.997
	(1.472)	(1.431)	(1.405)	(1.377)
N	163,763	88,471	176,896	136,203

Note: Means, Standard deviations in ( )s. Wage data in 1980 kr.
Source: Integrated Database for Labour Market Research (Danish IDA)

Table 2. Log of Hourly Wage Equations, 1983 and 1995: Fixed Effects Models

Specification	1983		1995	
	Female Coefficient	Proportion of the Gender Wage Gap "Explained"	Female Coefficient	Proportion of the Gender Wage Gap 'Explained'
Lnwage(female) – lnwage(male)	-.386	.000	-.341	.000
(1) Occupation fixed effects only	-.175	.547	-.168	.507
(2) Industry fixed effects only	-.379	.018	-.334	.021
(3) Establish. fixed effects only	-.382	.010	-.336	.015
(4) Job-cell fixed effects only	-.161	.583	-.156	.543
(5) Human capital-age only	-.278	.280	-.281	.176
(6) Human capital-age + Occupation fixed effects	-.163	.578	-.176	.484
(7) Human capital-age + Industry fixed effects	-.269	.303	-.266	.220
(8) Human capital-age + Establishment fixed effects	-.271	.298	-.273	.199
(9) Human capital-age + Job-cell fixed effects	-.148	.617	-.165	.516
(10) Human capital-exp only	-.272	.295	-.272	.202
(11) Human capital-exp + Occupation fixed effects	-.152	.606	-.162	.525
(12) Human capital-exp + Industry fixed effects	-.264	.316	-.259	.240
(13) Human capital-exp + Establishment fixed effects	-.263	.319	-.263	.229
(14) Human capital-exp + Job-cell fixed effects	-.137	.645	-.151	.557
N	252,234		313,099	

Note: Standard error on female coefficient = .001 for all specifications.
 1983 (1995): # of occupation fixed effects = 112 (119); # of industry fixed effects = 52 (52); # of establishment fixed effects = 2,109 (4,338); # of job-cell fixed effects = 30,160 (44,012).
 Human capital-age(exp) includes years of education, missing education dummy variable, age, age squared, (experience, experience squared), and province.

Table 3. Log of Hourly Wage Equations, 1983 and 1995: Fixed Effects Models--Comparison of Less Detailed and Detailed Occupation

| | 1983 | | 1995 | |
| | Female Coefficient | | Female Coefficient | |
Specification	Less Detailed	Detailed	Less Detailed	Detailed
Lnwage(female) – lnwage(male)	-.386	-.386	-.341	-.341
(1) Occupation fixed effects only	-.195	-.175	-.179	-.168
(2) Job-cell fixed effects only	-.176	-.161	-.167	-.156
(3) Human capital-age + Occupation fixed effects	-.186	-.163	-.191	-.176
(4) Human capital-age + Job-cell fixed effects	-.163	-.148	-.174	-.165
(5) Human capital-exp + Occupation fixed effects	-.176	-.152	-.178	-.162
(6) Human capital-exp + Job-cell fixed effects	-.153	-.137	-.161	-.151
N	252,234		313,099	

Note: Standard error on female coefficient = .001 for all specifications.

"Less detailed" column: 1983 (1995): # of occupation fixed effects = 30 (29); # of job-cell fixed effects = 21,101 (31,851).

"Detailed" column: 1983 (1995): # of occupation fixed effects = 112 (119); # of job-cell fixed effects = 30,160 (44,012).

Human capital-age(exp) includes years of education, missing education dummy variable, age, age squared, (experience, experience squared), and province.

Table 4. Log of Hourly Wage Equations, 1983: Proportion Female Models

Specification	Female	Occ.	Industry	Estab.	Job Cell	Proportion Of the Gender Wage Gap 'Explained'
			Proportion Female in:			
Lnwage(female) – lnwage(male)	-.386	---	---	---	---	.000
(1) Without human capital	-.173 (.002)	-.495 (.003)	---	---	---	.552
(2)	-.382 (.001)	---	-.041 (.005)	---	---	.010
(3)	-.383 (.001)	---	---	-.042 (.006)	---	.008
(4)	-.158 (.002)	---	---	---	-.439 (.003)	.591
(5)	-.162 (.002)	-.410 (.005)	.072 (.005)	.091 (.007)	-.114 (.005)	.580
(6) Human capital-age	-.159 (.001)	-.308 (.002)	---	---	---	.588
(7)	-.272 (.001)	---	-.081 (.004)	---	---	.295
(8)	-.273 (.001)	---	---	-.098 (.005)	---	.293
(9)	-.142 (.002)	---	---	---	-.284 (.002)	.632
(10)	-.143 (.002)	-.220 (.004)	.010 (.005)	.020 (.006)	-.108 (.004)	.630
(11) Human capital-exp	-.143 (.002)	-.342 (.002)	---	---	---	.630
(12)	-.265 (.001)	---	-.088 (.004)	---	---	.313
(13)	-.265 (.001)	---	---	-.126 (.005)	---	.313
(14)	-.125 (.002)	---	---	---	-.312 (.002)	.676
(15)	-.128 (.002)	-.259 (.004)	.021 (.005)	-.005 (.006)	-.101 (.004)	.668

Note: Standard error in ( )s. Sample size = 252,234.
 Human capital-age(exp) includes years of education, missing education dummy variable, age, age squared, (experience, experience squared), and province.

Table 5. Log of Hourly Wage Equations, 1995: Proportion Female Models

| Specification | Female | Proportion Female in: | | | | Proportion of the Gender Wage Gap 'Explained' |
		Occ.	Industry	Estab.	Job Cell	
Lnwage(female) – lnwage(male)	-.341	---	---	---	---	.000
(1) **Without human capital**	-.166 (.002)	-.494 (.003)	---	---	---	.513
(2)	-.336 (.001)	---	-.077 (.005)	---	---	.015
(3)	-.337 (.001)	---	---	-.062 (.006)	---	.012
(4)	-.155 (.002)	---	---	---	-.400 (.003)	.545
(5)	-.157 (.002)	-.437 (.004)	.051 (.006)	.100 (.006)	-.084 (.004)	.540
(6) **Human capital-age**	-.176 (.001)	-.321 (.002)	---	---	---	.484
(7)	-.267 (.001)	---	-.207 (.004)	---	---	.217
(8)	-.273 (.001)	---	---	-.135 (.005)	---	.199
(9)	-.163 (.001)	---	---	---	-.265 (.002)	.522
(10)	-.162 (.001)	-.262 (.004)	-.112 (.005)	.049 (.005)	-.063 (.004)	.525
(11) **Human capital-exp**	-.155 (.001)	-.363 (.002)	---	---	---	.545
(12)	-.258 (.001)	---	-.209 (.004)	---	---	.243
(13)	-.263 (.001)	---	---	-.155 (.005)	---	.229
(14)	-.142 (.001)	---	---	---	-.298 (.002)	.584
(15)	-.142 (.001)	-.306 (.004)	-.094 (.005)	.034 (.006)	-.062 (.004)	.584

Note: Standard error in ( )s. Sample size = 313,099.

Human capital-age(exp) includes years of education, missing education dummy variable, age, age squared, (experience, experience squared), and province.

Table 6. Log of Hourly Wage Equations, 1983 and 1995, Manufacturing Industry

Specification	Coefficient				Proportion of the Gender Wage Gap 'Explained'
		Proportion Female in:			
1983	Female	Occupation	Establish.	Job Cell	
Lnwage(female) – lnwage(male)	-.432	---	---	---	.000
(1) Without human capital	-.189 (.004)	-.462 (.009)	.155 (.014)	-.038 (.009)	.563
(2) Human capital-age	-.147 (.003)	-.285 (.008)	.062 (.013)	-.047 (.008)	.660
(3) Occupation fixed effects only	-.193 (.003)	---	---	---	.553
(4) Establishment fixed effects only	-.441 (.003)	---	---	---	-.021
(5) Job-cell fixed effects only	-.188 (.003)	---	---	---	.565
(6) Human capital-age + Job-cell fixed effects	-.149 (.003)	---	---	---	.655
1995					
Lnwage(female) – lnwage(male)	-.359	---	---	---	.000
(7) Without human capital	-.168 (.003)	-.427 (.008)	.471 (.012)	-.076 (.008)	.532
(8) Human capital-age	-.152 (.003)	-.279 (.007)	.223 (.011)	-.053 (.007)	.577
(9) Occupation fixed effects only	-.166 (.003)	---	---	---	.538
(10) Establishment fixed effects only	-.376 (.002)	---	---	---	-.047
(11) Job-cell fixed effects only	-.160 (.003)	---	---	---	.554
(12) Human capital-age + Job-cell fixed effects	-.151 (.003)	---	---	---	.579

Note: Standard error in ( )s. Sample size = 72,752 in 1983 and 86,242 in 1995.
  1983 (1995): # of occupation fixed effects = 97 (98); # of establishment fixed effects = 1,539 (2,485); # of job-cell fixed effects = 14,398 (19,722).
  Human capital-age includes years of education, missing education dummy variable, age, age squared, and province.

Table 7. Log of Hourly Wage Equations, 1983 and 1995, Wholesale and Retail Trade, Hotel, and Restaurant Industry

	Coefficient				Proportion of the Gender Wage Gap 'Explained'
Specification		Proportion Female in:			
1983	Female	Occupation	Establish.	Job Cell	
Lnwage(female) – lnwage(male)	-.399	---	---	---	.000
(1) Without human capital	-.177 (.004)	-.418 (.010)	.047 (.012)	-.138 (.010)	.556
(2) Human capital-age	-.161 (.003)	-.253 (.008)	-.087 (.010)	-.072 (.008)	.596
(3) Occupation fixed effects only	-.184 (.003)	---	---	---	.539
(4) Establishment fixed effects only	-.387 (.003)	---	---	---	.030
(5) Job-cell fixed effects only	-.176 (.003)	---	---	---	.559
(6) Human capital-age + Job-cell fixed effects	-.165 (.003)	---	---	---	.586
1995					
Lnwage(female) – lnwage(male)	-.374	---	---	---	.000
(7) Without human capital	-.176 (.004)	-.554 (.009)	-.233 (.012)	-.038 (.009)	.529
(8) Human capital-age	-.194 (.003)	-.390 (.008)	-.247 (.010)	.013 (.008)	.481
(9) Occupation fixed effects only	-.192 (.003)	---	---	---	.487
(10) Establishment fixed effects only	-.345 (.003)	---	---	---	.078
(11) Job-cell fixed effects only	-.181 (.003)	---	---	---	.516
(12) Human capital-age + Job-cell fixed effects	-.200 (.003)	---	---	---	.465

Note: Standard error in ( )s. Sample size = 65,692 in 1983 and 73,760 in 1995.

1983 (1995): # of occupation fixed effects = 90 (89); # of establishment fixed effects = 1,610 (2,837); # of job-cell fixed effects = 13,624 (17,652).

Human capital-age includes years of education, missing education dummy variable, age, age squared, and province.

Table 8. Log of Hourly Wage Equations, 1983 and 1995, Financial Intermediation and Business Activity Industry

Specification	Coefficient				Proportion of the Gender Wage Gap 'Explained'
		Proportion Female in:			
1983	Female	Occupation	Establish.	Job Cell	
Lnwage(female) – lnwage(male)	-.383	---	---	---	.000
(1) Without human capital	-.134 (.003)	-.511 (.010)	-.006 (.014)	-.103 (.009)	.650
(2) Human capital-age	-.135 (.003)	-.272 (.009)	.017 (.012)	-.105 (.008)	.648
(3) Occupation fixed effects only	-.146 (.003)	---	---	---	.619
(4) Establishment fixed effects only	-.368 (.003)	---	---	---	.039
(5) Job-cell fixed effects only	-.124 (.003)	---	---	---	.676
(6) Human capital-age + Job-cell fixed effects	-.130 (.002)	---	---	---	.661
1995					
Lnwage(female) – lnwage(male)	-.350	---	---	---	.000
(7) Without human capital	-.156 (.003)	-.570 (.008)	.003 (.011)	-.036 (.008)	.554
(8) Human capital-age	-.170 (.002)	-.352 (.007)	-.010 (.010)	-.030 (.007)	.514
(9) Occupation fixed effects only	-.160 (.002)	---	---	---	.543
(10) Establishment fixed effects only	-.329 (.002)	---	---	---	.060
(11) Job-cell fixed effects only	-.151 (.002)	---	---	---	.569
(12) Human capital-age + Job-cell fixed effects	-.166 (.002)	---	---	---	.526

Note: Standard error in ( )s. Sample size = 61,185 in 1983 and 78,116 in 1995.
  1983 (1995): # of occupation fixed effects = 95 (94); # of establishment fixed effects = 1,069 (1,681); # of job-cell fixed effects = 8,236 (12,129).
  Human capital-age includes years of education, missing education dummy variable, age, age squared, and province.

Appendix Table 1. Selection of Sample

	1983		1995	
	Males	Females	Males	Females
N private sector salaried workers	310,179	276,174	329,977	301,899
1. Drop missing industry	2,571	4,489	63	40
2. Drop part-time workers	70,228	139,208	68,655	102,791
N used to create proportion female in occupation, industry, establishment, and job cell	237,380	132,477	261,259	199,068
3. Drop age <18 or age > 65	1,305	412	676	141
4. Drop establishment size < 20	60,393	40,065	60,931	52,628
5. Drop unreliable wage information	1,037	355	2,384	1,467
6. Drop job cell = 1	10,882	3,174	20,372	8,629
N used in estimations	163,763	88,471	176,896	136,203
	252,234		313,099	

Appendix Table 2. Correlation Matrix of Proportion Female Variables, 1983 and 1995

	1983			
	Proportion Female in:			
	Occupation	Industry	Establishment	Job Cell
Occupation	1.000	---	---	---
Industry	.290	1.000	---	---
Establishment	.251	.528	1.000	---
Job Cell	.910	.339	.336	1.000
	1995			
Occupation	1.000	---	---	---
Industry	.279	1.000	---	---
Establishment	.268	.518	1.000	---
Job Cell	.873	.326	.373	1.000

Note: Sample size = 252,234 in 1983 and 313,099 in 1995.

www.ingramcontent.com/pod-product-compliance
Lightning Source LLC
Chambersburg PA
CBHW081417170526
45166CB00010B/3378